This Letter Tracing Workbook Belongs To

_____

Part One
Tracing letters

In this part you have all letters to trace and practice how to write curving letters

B

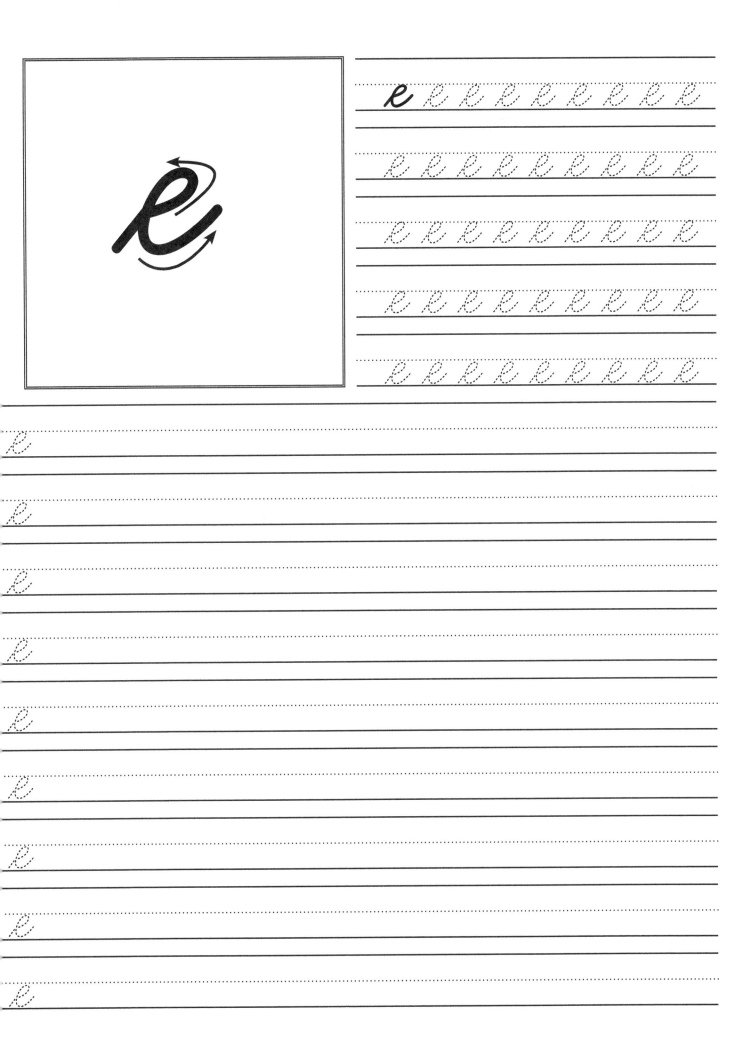

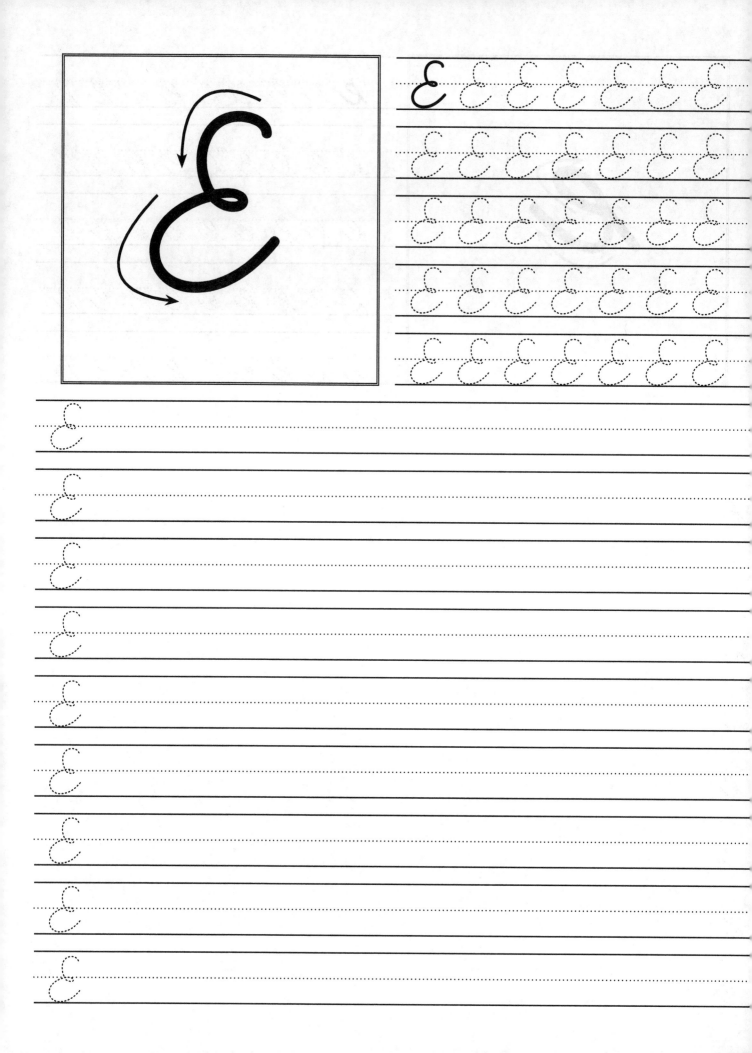

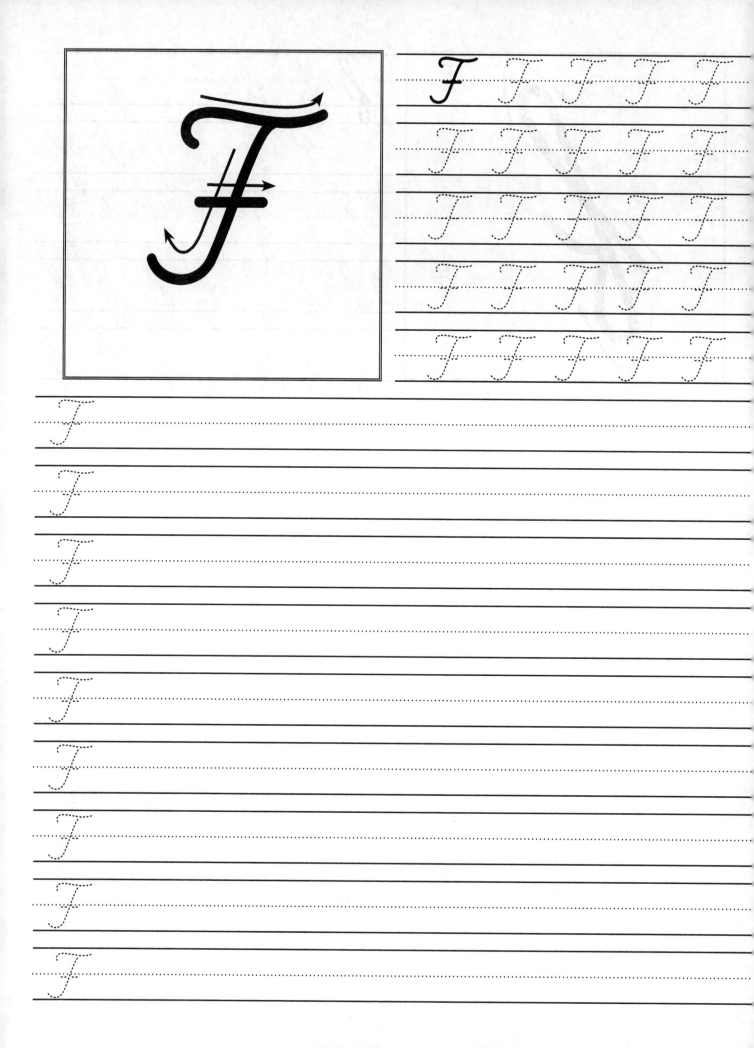

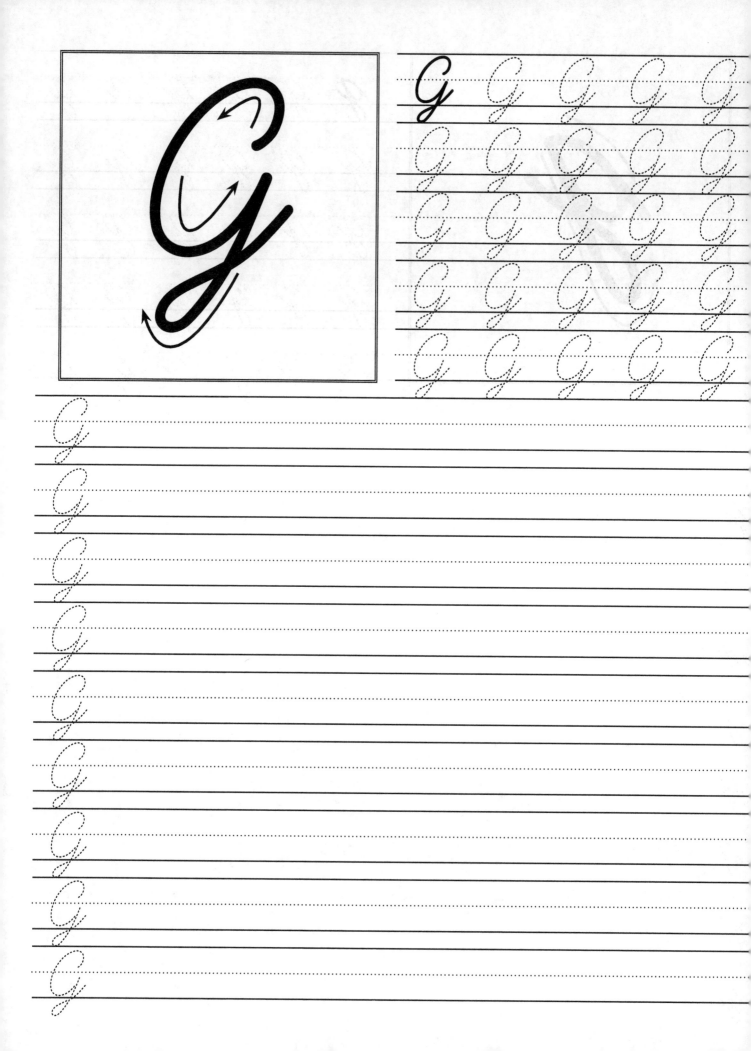

H

i

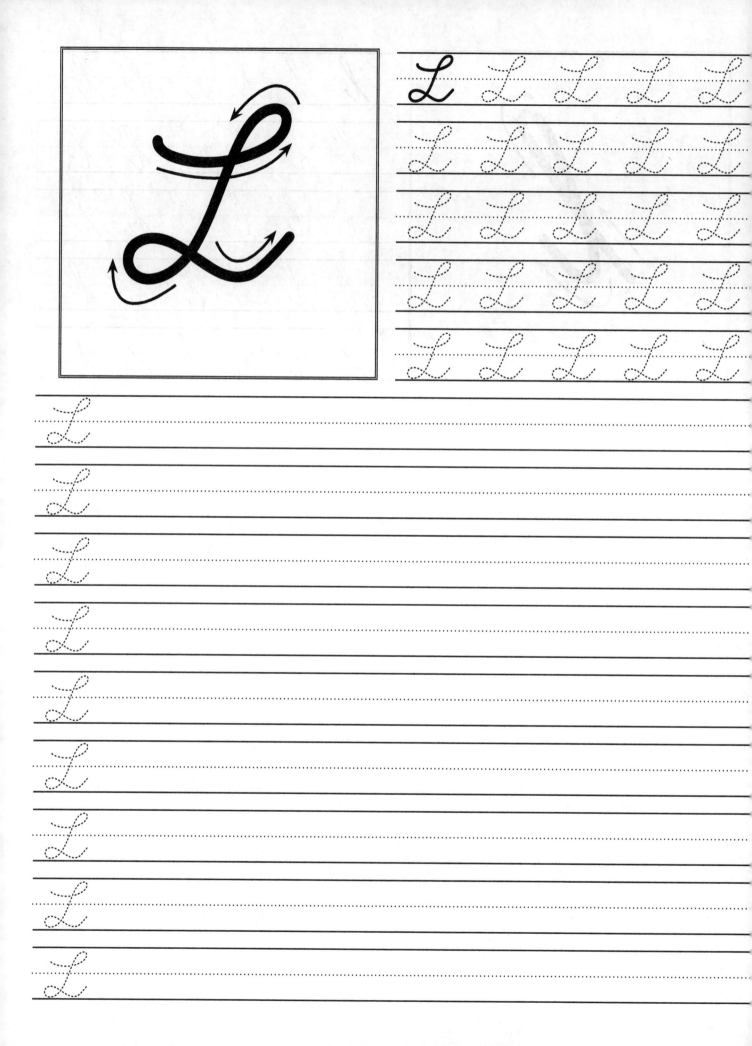

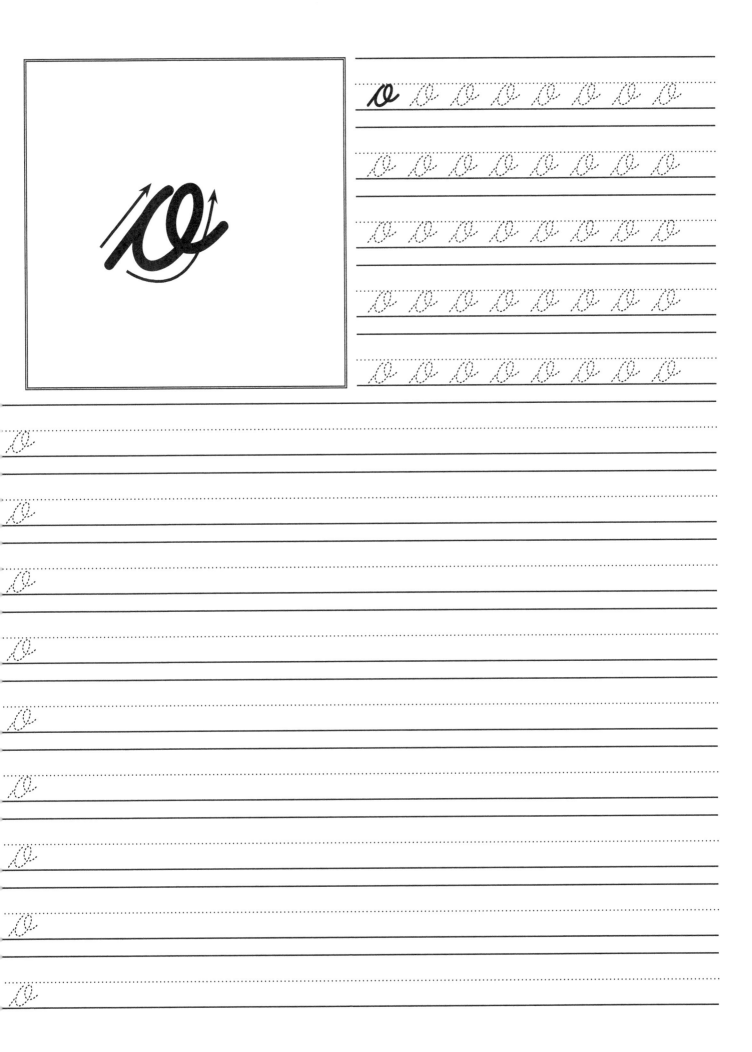

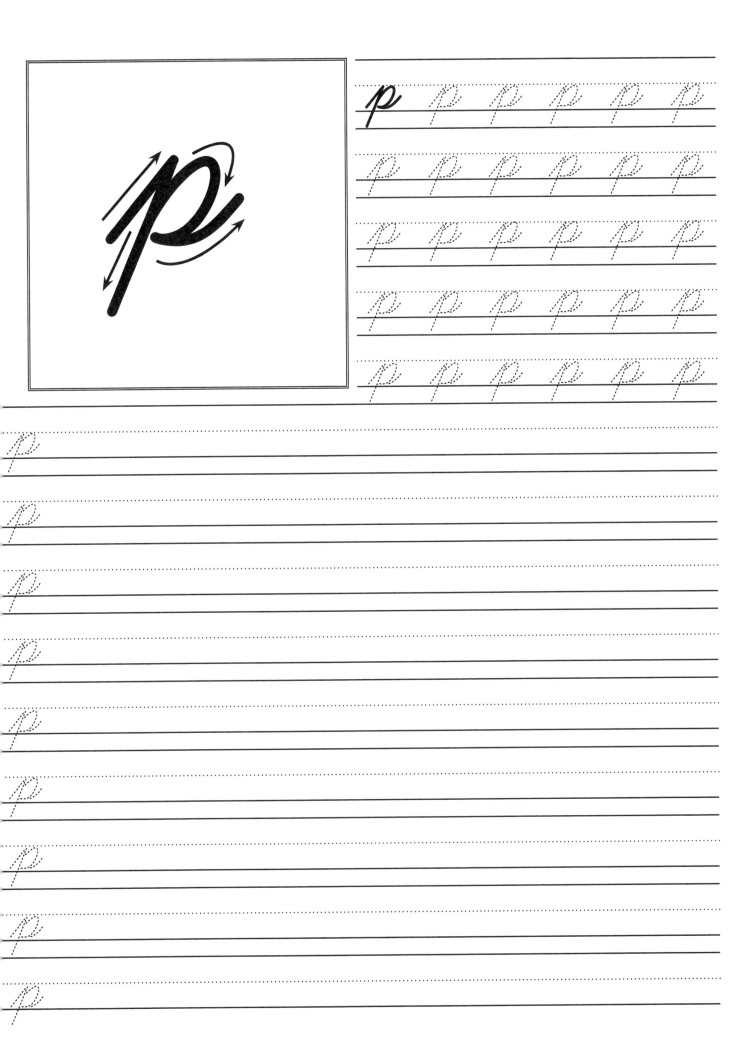

U

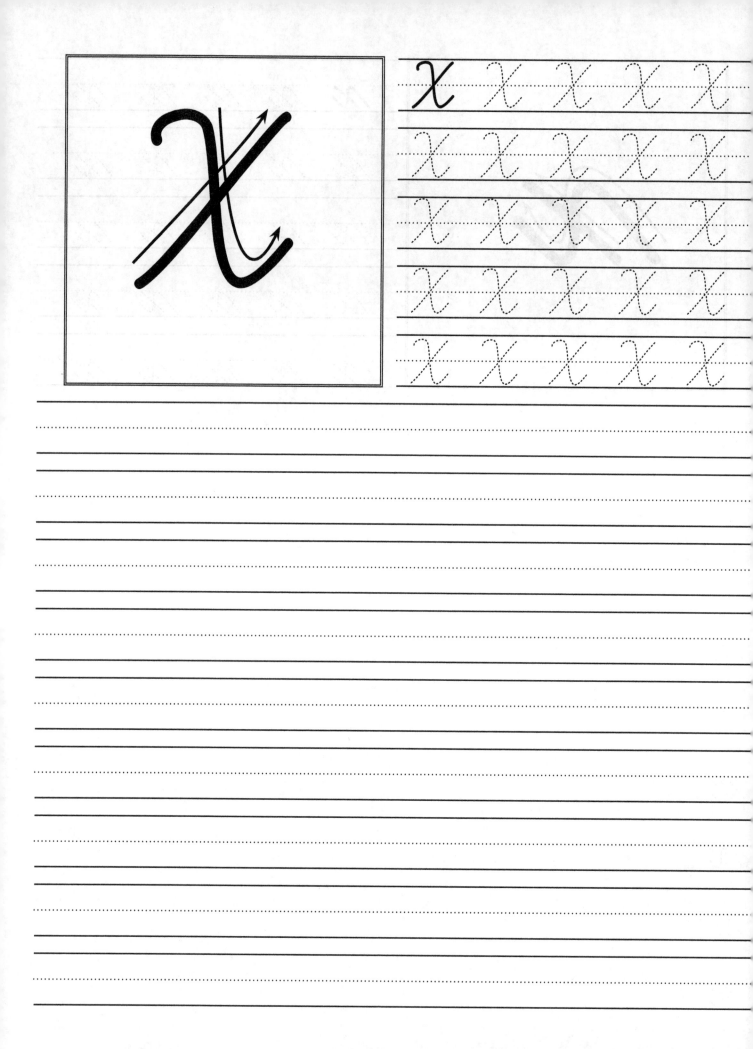

Part Two
Tracing Words

In this part you have a collection of curving words to practice connecting two curving letters and more

understand *understand*

ice *ice*

precede *precede*

punish *punish*

prisoner *prisoner*

frown *frown*

provincial *provincial*

hold

freedom

men

dependence

neighbor

acually

minister

every *every*

beneath *beneath*

drive *drive*

tree *tree*

boat *boat*

arraseed *arraseed*

junior *junior*

mentioned

information

governor

stands

word

note

student

ordered *ordered*

meaning *meaning*

cermony *cermony*

hence *hence*

material *material*

speak *speak*

right *right*

soft

providen

stair

lower

tarry

leeward

egg

here here

spite spite

horse horse

comb comb

snake snake

letter letter

camera camera

elephant elephant

elevator elevator

book book

flag flag

hammer hammer

sponge sponge

bell bell

shop shop

tortoise tortoise

shoe shoe

nose nose

burger burger

balloon balloon

telephone telephone

pencil pencil

tree tree

mouse mouse

television television

lawyer lawyer

bee bee

rain rain

fire *fire*

bath *bath*

aeroplane *aeroplane*

guitar *guitar*

paint *paint*

carpet *carpet*

song *song*

money money

knife knife

vote vote

rocket rocket

mountain mountain

car car

ladder ladder

glue *glue*

cat *cat*

radio *radio*

table *table*

heart *heart*

trap *trap*

key *key*

matchstick matchstick

copier copier

cactuse cactuse

prison prison

flower flower

string string

eraser eraser

gun *gun*

pin *pin*

jungle *jungle*

super *super*

rice *rice*

liberty *liberty*

mango *mango*

duster *duster*

enchanting *enchanting*

dance *dance*

duck *duck*

modi *modi*

star *star*

biscuit *biscuit*

umbrella *umbrella*

rocking *rocking*

band *band*

pain *pain*

swimming *swimming*

neck *neck*

desk *desk*

stand stand

lorry lorry

tiger tiger

dell dell

sing sing

ocean ocean

religion religion

mouth mouth

champion champion

cupboard cupboard

speaker speaker

walking walking

gate gate

room room

computer *computer*

ball *ball*

rope *rope*

festival *festival*

switch *switch*

finger *finger*

banana *banana*

eye eye

sweet sweet

razor razor

table table

london london

cricket cricket

crown crown

ant ant

glass glass

oil oil

wind wind

floor floor

carbon carbon

wonderful wonderful

pen *pen*

cell *cell*

stereo *stereo*

comedy *comedy*

tv *tv*

den *den*

leech *leech*

exraordinary *exraordinary*

simple *simple*

learn *learn*

meditate *meditate*

iron *iron*

box *box*

stove *stove*

Part Three
Tracing Sentences

In this part you have a collection of motivate curving quotes to practice to write full sentences

Why stop dreaming when you are awake

Why stop dreaming when you are awake

Say yes more than no

Say yes more than no

The only time you should look back, is to see how far you've come

If you were looking for a sign, this is it

If you were looking for a sign

this is it

"I am in charge of how I feel and today I am choosing happiness

Good things come to those who wait work their asses off and never give up

If you're making mistakes it means you're out there doing something

Give your best everyday

Give your best everyday

Dream. Believe. Do. Repeat

Dream. Believe. Do. Repeat

Dream. Believe. Do. Repeat

Be the type of person you want

to meet

Replace thoughts of worry with thoughts of hope, faith, and victory

I can't afford to hate anyone.
I don't have that kind of time

I can't afford to hate anyone.
I don't have that kind of time

Strong is what happens when you run out of weak

Integrity is doing the right
thing when no one is watching

Integrity is doing the right
thing when no one is watching

I will persist until I succeed

Keep calm because this too shall pass

Keep calm because this too shall pass

Fear has two meanings! The choice is yours

Fear has two meanings! The choice is yours

It is not the mountain we conquer, but ourselves

It is not the mountain we conquer, but ourselves

Life is too short to live the same day twice

Life is too short to live the

same day twice

Don't judge me by my past.
I don't live there anymore

Don't judge me by my past.
I don't live there anymore

I am not beautiful like you.
I'm beautiful like me

A true love story never ends

A true love story never ends

A change may be just around the corner

A change may be just around the corner

BE YOUR OWN HERO

BE YOUR OWN HERO

Be yourself, everyone else is taken

Be yourself, everyone else is taken

Do something that your future self will thank you for

Do something that your future self will thank you for

The time is: NOW

The time is: NOW

The time is: NOW

Fear is a lair

Fear is a lair

Believing in yourself is the first seret to seccess

Believing in yourself is the

first seret to seccess